His Drums Fell Silent, the Voices Still Speak

A Mother and Son's Journey with Mental Illness through the Mental Health System . . . and Beyond

Judyth Thomas

WestBow
PRESS
A DIVISION OF THOMAS NELSON
& ZONDERVAN

WestBow Press books may be ordered through booksellers or by contacting:

WestBow Press
A Division of Thomas Nelson & Zondervan
1663 Liberty Drive
Bloomington, IN 47403
www.westbowpress.com
1 (866) 928-1240

Because of the dynamic nature of the Internet, any web addresses or links contained in this book may have changed since publication and may no longer be valid. The views expressed in this work are solely those of the author and do not necessarily reflect the views of the publisher, and the publisher hereby disclaims any responsibility for them.

Any people depicted in stock imagery provided by Thinkstock are models, and such images are being used for illustrative purposes only. Certain stock imagery © Thinkstock.

All Scripture quotations in this publications are from The Message. Copyright © by Eugene H. Peterson 1993, 1994, 1995, 1996, 2000, 2001, 2002. Used by permission of NavPress Publishing Group.

ISBN: 978-1-4908-3938-7 (sc)
ISBN: 978-1-4908-3940-0 (hc)
ISBN: 978-1-4908-3939-4 (e)

Library of Congress Control Number: 2014909834

Printed in the United States of America.

WestBow Press rev. date: 08/04/2014

This story is dedicated to:

Jon David Miller

and

Rachel Elizabeth Miller
Jaren David Miller
Hasia Rose Miller

Contents

Acknowledgements

Without the following people, this story would never have unfolded as it has and would certainly never been told. Mine has been a long journey—over thirty years. The first ten years I walked with my son, Jon David, as he struggled with his mental illness. These past twenty-two years I have served with joy my friends who also struggle with mental illness by founding and working with Ladder Homes, a non-profit organization that provides appropriate, affordable housing and case management support.

Obviously, in such a long span of time, there are many persons I must acknowledge. Words cannot express my gratitude for those listed below as well as those whose names are not included—those who have touched my life, Jon David's life, and the life of Ladder Homes. I hope and trust you know who you are and how important you are to me.

Above all else, I must acknowledge God's presence and activity in this story I am telling. God's comfort, love, and faithfulness have given me the strength I have needed to live through the pain and agony reflected in this story. God's voice and guidance have provided the vision and success resulting in Ladder Homes. God's unconditional love for those children struggling with mental illness is surely the foundation for all that we do.

When we first moved back to Holland after twenty years living in Ohio, I discovered the Ottawa County Chapter of N.A.M.I. (National Alliance for the Mentally Ill), a support group for family and friends of adult children with mental illness. It was a safe place where we could share our frustrations and pain as well as victories. Helen Brownson led the group, and I am grateful to her and the other members for their support in the midst of my own journey. It was also a committee of the group which led to the formation of Ladder Homes. Joyce Kortman, Executive Director of H.O.M.E. (Housing Opportunities Made Equitable) was instrumental in supporting us until our organization was on its feet.

Gretchen Nale was by my side, journeying with me through the times of pain and frustration. She was a major player in the early years of Ladder Homes and continues to be on the Board of Directors.

I can never thank my friend from Ohio, Pam D'huyvetter, for her presence in my life during the summer of 1991. She moved up with me and spent three months sleeping on my couch and just being available as I needed her. Thank you, Pam, for your love and for encouraging me to write this story.

To Sue Van Peursem, former Case Manager, and Jonathan Book, Executive Director/Case Manager of Ladder Homes. Your dedication and passion for the program and our residents have warmed my heart. You love the residents. They love you. And that has made all the difference. The past and present members of the

Ladder Board of Directors have faithfully kept our organization healthy and successful.

So many friends and members of my family have been there for me, for Jon David, and for Ladder. Your support has loved me through the rough times and challenges during the past thirty years.

Donald and Martha Thomas (my parents): for loving your daughter and grandson so deeply and so well.

John and Jim Thomas and Janet Thomas-Kobes (my siblings): for being supportive and loving aunts, uncles, and siblings.

Pam Carey and Sharon Wright: for all the prayers, conversations, and so many trips from Columbus to Holland. My spiritual sisters, I love you both so very much.

B.J. Berghorst, Lois Carder, Audrianne Hill, and Brad Williams: for all the Saturday morning breakfasts, road trips, holiday get-togethers, and faithful friendships

Libby and John Bosman: for your being the best, most supportive neighbors one could ever wish for.

Hope College Theatre faculty, staff and students: for your support and love as my second family. To share each day with you for twenty-five years always lifted my spirits and helped me meet the challenges of life.

The writing of this story has been a labor of love for me and for many others.

Eleanor Brunsell: my "detail person." I could not have finished this book without you. You lovingly pushed me forward when I was discouraged. You edited my writing and gave me constructive feedback, allowing me to let my writing flow. Thank you, also, for co-founding Ladder Homes with me.

Margaret (Peg) Van Grouw: for your editing skills and your ideas that spurred on my writing.

A very special thank you to my brother Jim who pushed me deeper and farther than I ever thought I could go.

Foreword

There are two stories I must tell. One is the story of my son Jon David. The other is the story of Ladder Homes. And I cannot tell one without the other as they are so intertwined. To understand the Ladder story, one must get to know my son, a representative in a way of all those people who struggle with mental illness and their families who have inspired the mission of Ladder Homes.

It started during Jon's junior year of high school—this disease that changed his and our family's life. It was a frightening, frustrating, painful journey for all of us—but especially for him.

I was taking my daily walk one morning this past summer when all of a sudden the tears began to flow. I saw in my mind's eye your sweet little toddler's face, my son, and realized that I didn't appreciate you back then…when you were a baby, a toddler, a young boy, a young man. I was too busy being a single mom with two small children, teaching full time, taking care of business. Oh, I loved you—no doubt about that. I just didn't hug you enough, kiss you enough, How could I know back then that your later years would be so devastating? How could I know that your dreams and my dreams for you would not come true?

As I write your story and the story of Ladder Homes, your legacy, the memories come flooding back. Some bring tears, others smiles. I thank God for the years I did have with the healthy you. At the same time I remember screaming at God "Why have you allowed my son to experience such pain? If I believe you are able to heal him, how could I not be angry with you for not doing so?"

I do not know the answer to these questions. Someday I will. But for now I travel the road in front of me, trusting that the voices that still speak will bring a better quality of life for the friends of mine who struggle with mental illness and a sense of peace for their family and friends. It is in believing that my pain and Jon David's pain can result in a better life for others that I find my peace.

The purpose of this project is twofold. The story of Jon and my journey is one which is replicated by millions of families all over our country. I hope this book will speak to them and let them know they are not alone and maybe give them some knowledge, insight, and options to make their journey easier and more effective than ours was. I also hope that it will educate society as to what it is like to be mentally ill and how devastating the journey is for their families and friends.

I write about Ladder Homes to possibly inspire others to duplicate our program for their children who need the housing and support to improve their quality of life. The supportive independent housing that we provide works, and we hope to encourage others to try it. You can do it!!

Part I

Jon David's Early Years:
My All-American Son

My choice is you, God, first and only.
And now I find I'm your choice.
You set me up with a house and yard.
And then you made me your heir!
Now you've got my feet on the path,
All radiant from the shining of your face.
Ever since you took my hand,
I'm on the right way.
Psalms 16:5-6. 11

<u>Chapter 1</u>

In late August of 1966 my husband and I moved to New Orleans. He had received a fellowship in theatre to Tulane University. At the time I was eight and a half months pregnant, looking forward to my first child. I was scared—I had no family or friends in the area and had no doctor. I had had no prenatal care and was totally ignorant in terms of childbirth. But I was young and, with the innocence/ignorance of the young I trusted that things would work out. And they did. Jon David was born on September 23, a healthy, beautiful baby.

About a week after Jon was born, my husband quit Tulane, saying it wasn't as good a program as he thought it would be. We ended up flying back north, and over the next two years we lived at both our parents' houses and several different apartments. Finally he got an assistantship in theatre at The Ohio State University, and we moved to Columbus where the children and I lived for the next twenty years. During all this time Jon remained healthy and happy, seeming to adjust well to all the moves and chaos of our lives.

One of the pictures in my mind is of Jon when he was about two. He had on a sailor hat and was lying down on the ground, his nose to the pavement. "Mommy," he said. "Come here and look at this." I walked over and saw a huge anthill crowded with ants. Even then he was a curious soul, excited about learning and experiencing new things…even the ants!

Jon's father and I separated when Jon was about two years old. Jon and I moved to Holland so I could finish my B.A. at Hope College. I received my degree and a teaching certificate while taking care of Jon and being pregnant with his sister Rachel. We lived in an apartment right next to the train tracks. At first, when the train went by in the middle of the night, Jon would wake up scared. But it wasn't long before he got used to it and became enthralled with trains. He always wanted to go out and watch them go by—even in the rain and snow! Jon adjusted well to the changes in his life and continued to be a joy.

Chapter 2

During the semester I was in school Jon's father and I decided to get back together mostly because I was pregnant. So Jon and I moved back to Columbus at the end of the semester. I had applied for and received a teaching position with the Columbus Public Schools to start in the fall. Rachel was born in July, and a few weeks later their father left for good. Fortunately I now had a good job and was able to support our little family.

Jon's father and I met in Greece. We were both American student ambassadors in an exchange program. I was young and naïve and fell madly in love. Looking back, a wiser me would have realized that it should have remained a summer romance that ended as summer ended. From the beginning the marriage was not a healthy, sustainable one. Over the four years of marriage I gradually realized that it had been lust, not love that attracted us to each other. By the time of the divorce I was relieved, not hurt.

It always appeared to me that the children adjusted well to the frequent changes in our lives. Over the years, however, I have wondered if the changes/chaos and absence of a father affected Jon's later life. I tried my best to give them a stable life following the divorce, but perhaps a father who was present (regardless of the divorce) would have made a difference. I don't know. I do know that schizophrenia is a chemical imbalance in the brain—a physical disorder, not an emotional one. But perhaps a more stable life with a father present would have reduced the severity of Jon's illness.

Unfortunately in the years to follow there was very little contact with the children's father or his side of the family. I tried to keep in touch, make the children available to them, but they seemed not to care. I have never figured out why, since they were good people. So the children's extended family was my family, and how much Jon and Rachel loved spending time with them in Michigan. Many weekends I loaded them up in our blue Volkswagen bug and drove the five hours to Holland to spend the weekend with Grandma and Grandpa. We spent summer weeks and vacations there, when Jon and Rachel spent time with their aunts, uncles, and cousins, playing, laughing, and just fooling around. They especially enjoyed their time with Aunt Jan, my younger sister. They were always finding stupid, silly things to say and do and would laugh until their stomachs hurt.

When Jon David was about 5 years old, we took one of our trips to Holland. It was Easter and a very cold day. As I came over a hill, there was a line of cars, all pulled over by the state troopers for speeding. Unfortunately I became one of those waiting in line. Because our VW bug had no heat unless we were moving, the car soon became freezing. When the officer finally reached us, he took pity on us (a car with a baby, a toddler, and no heat) and just gave me a warning. All the rest of way to Holland Jon's little chin rested on my shoulder (this was prior to seat belts), his eyes on the speedometer making sure I wasn't speeding. If he saw that I was going even a mile over the speed limit, he would anxiously say, "Mommy, slow down!" Fortunately we made it to Holland without being stopped again, thanks in great part to my co-pilot little Jon David.

When Jon was in kindergarten I got a call from his teacher. She was concerned that Jon might have a hearing problem. I told her I hadn't noticed anything. But as I thought about it, I realized that I was having to raise my voice to him. I guess I just thought he wasn't listening to me, although he had never before given me any problems. I took him to the doctor, and it was discovered that he had liquid built up and needed tubes put in his ears. I'll never forget our ride back home after the surgery. First of all, the Volkswagen bug was kind of a noisy car. Also we were driving on the freeway with lots of cars whizzing by. "Oh, my gosh, Mommy, it's so noisy!" said Jon, his eyes big and excited. I felt so bad that my son had gone for a time not hearing well and I didn't notice it. But now he was excited about his new world of sound!

Chapter 3

Jon David and I also had three step brothers. For the most part we all got along, but there were times when that dynamic would play a role in the family and we became a dysfunctional family. With both of our sensitive spirits, there were times we just couldn't take the chaos. I had temper tantrums and screamed and yelled and fought one of the boys it seemed every day. Never Jon David though.

-Rachel's Voice

When Jon was seven and Rachel was four I married a man who had three sons. Prior to our marriage the boys lived with their mother and spent every other weekend with us. The five children seemed to get along well and we tried our best to adjust to the situation. One day the boys' mother just dropped the boys off at our house and said she couldn't take care of them anymore. So there I was going from a working mother of two to a stay-at-home mother of five (ages four to ten). Quite an adjustment! It was a time when little was written or spoken of regarding the "blended" family (a term not even used then). At times it was a struggle as we tried to treat all the children equally. In all of it, my husband was a good stepfather. Looking back, I believe I was less a good stepmother. We did our best without the knowledge and guidance that is available today. During it all Jon and Rachel became very close. Often times it seemed that it was the two of them against the boys. A strong sister/brother bond formed during these years and lasted into adulthood.

The children were all involved in sports—soccer, softball, basketball, football. Jon especially liked and did well in football and basketball. What he *didn't* like was prior to soccer season when my husband had all five of the children run around the block a number of times every day to get them in shape. It was certainly not Jon's favorite time of the day!

Chapter 4

Remembering my brother, Jon David Miller, is a mixed bag of emotions. The memories of our childhood—so much fun, playing music with him and recording ourselves on tape cassettes, and rewinding them over and over and just belly laughing. The memories of him and the drum line and me on the dance team and the lights on in the stadium—knowing we were both out there together. Then there was his election to the homecoming court, and because of that my mother escorted him onto the field, so there we were, all of us under the lights. I have no better memory than that night. It was an overwhelming feeling of joy

-Rachel's Voice

Jon got good grades, chose good, solid friends, was very popular (even chosen to be on the King's Court his junior year). When he reached high school he gave up sports to be involved in the band and orchestra. He never got in trouble—well, almost never. Jon David had an active social life. His girlfriend, Melissa, was a constant throughout his high school years. One of my favorite pictures is that of Jon David and Melissa all dressed up in black with red bow ties and cummerbunds for a dance. They were such a handsome couple and really made each other happy. As most parents, I was a little worried about their becoming too close at a young age. But I really liked Melissa, and they seemed to be good for each other.

When Jon was nominated for King's Court, he had to give a speech on the person in his life that inspired him. He chose my grandfather, his great grandfather. He was a coach of a successful football team in a small town in upstate New York. When he came to visit us in Holland, he would gather the children around him and "preach" to them about life and life's lessons. He spoke about never giving up, about picking oneself up and keeping on. Jon took those lessons into his own life and always remembered Grandpa Morgan's "lessons." He was not a public speaker and was very nervous. But he did a fine job, and I was proud of him.

Jon also had a group of good, fun-loving "guy" friends who were in the band and orchestra with him and with whom he spent a great deal of time. Every Friday night after a football game, they had a band party at someone's house. I always called the parents to make sure they would be home to supervise. At some point, I found out that the parents often didn't do much supervising, so when Jon wanted a party at our house I agreed but told him I would be up in my room and would check on them occasionally. "Absolutely no beer in the house", I said.

There must have been at least 50 kids in the house and out in the yard that night. I dutifully checked on them and everything seemed fine—no beer that I could see. The next morning I went outside and found to my horror beer cans covering the front and back yard. There indeed had been no beer in the house—just outside the house! Jon spent most of the morning cleaning up the yard. (This was one of those "almost never a problem" times.) And I thought I was such a smart mother!!

Chapter 5

Jon David's passion was the drums. Ever since he could hold two sticks in his little hands he was drumming on everything and anything. He was a percussionist at age two! I remember his saying, "Mommy, do you have anything I can drum on?" Over the early years he went through coffee cans, oatmeal boxes, and every kind of box we could come up with. I never threw anything away that he could use! When he was about four years old Santa Clause brought him a child's drum set. "Oh, I love, love Santa," Jon said with sparkling eyes and a huge smile. We placed the set up in his bedroom, and he spent hours playing his drums to the sounds of the Jackson Five and the Partridge Family. He was in his glory.

At this time we were living in a townhouse in Columbus, Ohio. One day I was outside talking to the two young men who were our neighbors. They asked me, "What record are you playing with the drums?" Thinking they were unhappy with the loud music, I told them to let me know when it bothered them. They said, "No, that's not it. We just love the music. What record is it?" When I told them it was Jon playing the drums, they couldn't believe that such music was coming from the little boy who they were used to seeing riding around on his big wheel or throwing the ball to his friends in the neighborhood.

> *Of course there were the times that we grooved to Michael Jackson and the rock band Kiss. One hour of his practice everyday after school. I went crazy most of the time, but he was so good and would listen to a number of genres of music. I learned about jazz, blues, rock, rhythm and blues and Motown. Musical education I would use later in life and would always thank Jon for teaching me those things.*
>
> *-Rachel's Voice*

I have to admit that Jon's drumming drove his sister and me batty at times. Whenever we were in the car he was "pounding" on the dashboard or the seat. It seemed that music was inside of him and had to come out no matter where he was. I believe it was a gift that couldn't be denied from the time he was two.

As Jon David grew older he took a few drum lessons and eventually joined every orchestra and band he could. He was a paper boy for years and saved enough money to eventually buy himself a great drum set which "lived" in every basement of every house we lived in. By the time he got to high school, he was the top percussionist in the band and orchestra and won a number of regional and state awards. I remember one concert when in the middle of a song the director walked off stage and allowed Jon to play his drums for about five minutes. He got a standing ovation from the audience. What a solo that was!

His goal was to apply to The Ohio State University and try out for the marching band. His dream was to spend his life with his drums. He often said," I don't know how I can make a living as a percussionist, but I have to believe that it will happen." My Jon was intelligent, talented, creative, and handsome--a young man any mother could be proud of. And I was.

Jon David and his ants!

My little Dutch boy

Jon David, Mom, Rachel Elizabeth

Batter up!

My football hero!

Jon David the percussionist

Jon David's high school graduation

Jon David...in thought

Part II

Jon David's Later Years: My Son's Broken Brain

God, listen! Listen to my prayer,
Listen to the pain in my cries.
Don't turn your back on me
Just when I need you so desperately.
Pay attention! This is a cry for help!
And hurry—this can't wait!
-Psalms 102:1-2

Chapter 6

Jon did receive a scholarship to OSU, but his goal was shattered by the onset of his mental illness. While he continued to play his drums--the only thing that gave him any joy--he was unable to move ahead with his life. It was devastating for him as he realized his dream was not to be. As the illness progressed, he was unable to continue his relationships with Melissa and the rest of his friends. They tried to be there for him, but eventually they fell away as he became a hermit, spending all his time in his room, isolated and depressed.

During his junior year Jon David began to exhibit some health problems. He dropped out of all activities, and his grades fell. He became isolated and withdrawn. He had headaches and complained that his head was swelling. His sinuses bothered him. Then he had black stools and spent a week in the hospital where the doctors could find nothing wrong. We went to neurologists, ears/ nose/throat specialists, internists—every kind of doctor who just might have an answer for these growing problems.

In the meantime Jon spent hours reading up on vitamins and regulating his diet to include specific ones. He fasted for days at a time. He researched books, including the Bible, for answers. He spent every day trying to figure out what was wrong with him. We went to a dermatologist who suggested that his symptoms might be due to allergies, perhaps a brain allergy. My parents even flew us down to Dallas to a hospital that dealt exclusively with brain allergies. Unfortunately by this time Jon was just too ill to follow the program, and we came back with no answers.

At this point I began to think that all these physical ailments might be caused by some emotional problems. At the time I was pretty much ignorant of mental illness. By now Jon was living in the basement like a hermit, never showering or brushing his teeth, never going to school during his senior year. (He tried but always came home saying his headaches were just too bad to stay in class.) He had what we called his "fits," yelling and screaming in his room as though he were trying to push out some pain that was inside of him.

During these times Jon David often destroyed items in his room. Once I walked in after one of his "fits" and found his guitar smashed to pieces. He never did, however, destroy anyone else's possessions. He seldom ate and never at the table with the family. His hair grew long, and he covered his face with it. He cried and my heart broke. I didn't know how to help him My beautiful boy had descended into such a dark place, and I didn't know how to fix whatever was wrong with him

One day I came upstairs from doing the laundry to find Jon in the kitchen brandishing a knife. To this day I don't know what he was planning on doing with it. But I was scared for him and me. I called the police, but by the time they arrived, Jon was curled up in a fetal position on the floor. The police couldn't do anything since he was by then not threatening to harm himself or anyone else. That night I lay in my bed and cried out to God, "God, help me, help my son! I don't know what to do to help him. There's something so wrong with him and I don't know what to do. Please, please send me an answer and bring some peace to me and to my son."

About the time Jon's illness began to manifest itself, his stepfather was diagnosed with the first of several brain tumors, and he had surgery to remove it. One day after he returned home, he and Jon got into an argument (I don't remember what it was about). Jon ran up a few steps, turned around and kicked his stepfather, who was following him, in the head. Although the only injury he inflicted was a cut lip, all Jon saw was the blood. He left the house in panic and ran about five miles to his biological father's house, believing he had killed his stepfather. He was scared to death. Jon and his stepfather were really very close, which made the situation even worse for Jon. He eventually returned home to continue his lonely, painful journey.

His darkness fell over our house. His stepfather spent more and more time at work. He sister began to run with the wrong crowd just to be away from the house and her big brother whom she loved so much. She couldn't stand to see him so ill. And I carried his pain with mine day after day, week after week, month after month. I, too, was lonely in my pain. Where would I find the answers? *Could* I find the answers? Was there anyone out there who could help?

> *Then the darkness came in. Oh how I couldn't take what was happening to my brother. "What was going on," I would say to my mother constantly. Night after night of him screaming and throwing himself around his bedroom. What was this horror?*
>
> *-Rachel's Voice*

Chapter 7

In 1984, during the summer after Jon's senior year, we decided to send him to Holland to spend some time with his grandparents. He loved them so much and had always enjoyed being with them. I had hoped that maybe a change of scenery would help. He was up there for two days when I got a call from my mother. He was holing up in their basement and exhibiting the same behaviors as he had at home. So I drove the five hours to my parents' house. We put Jon in the car and drove him to a nearby psychiatric hospital where he was admitted for observation. The doctors said he would be in the hospital for at least several weeks, so I drove back to Columbus to await their diagnosis and take care of the difficult situations at home.

I'll never forget the day I got the call from the psychiatrist. I was sitting on my bed when he said "schizophrenia." While I did not know much about mental illness, I recognized that word and knew at once that this was a serious diagnosis. The doctor indicated that it was most likely he could never hold down a full-time job or have a family. My heart broke. I fell on my bed holding my stomach, holding myself, wailing for my precious little boy. The doctor's words kept reverberating in my head: "no real future, no family, no productive job." No pill could cure him. "One third of people with schizophrenia," said the doctor," would spend most of their lives hospitalized, one-third would be severely disabled, and one third might be able to manage some sort of meaningful lives." I cried for hours. The dreams I had for my son were shattered. I could only imagine how he would feel when he finally realized that *his* dreams were not to be.

Jon David remained in the hospital for seven months, during which time he was put on multiple strong anti-psychotic medication to no avail. From what I could tell, they didn't even wean him off of one medication before they put him on another. When I visited him, he was like a zombie—emotionless, withdrawn, quiet. The doctors said he seldom interacted with others. Of course not! He was so medicated he could hardly keep his head up.

During one of my visits, I met with his therapist. He informed me that he had "fired" (he actually used that term) Jon because he refused to talk about his family. Apparently this older man was still working under the assumption that mental illness was caused by some sort of family disfunction, especially regarding the mother. Jon had informed him that whatever was wrong with him had nothing to do with his family and he would not talk about it. I informed this therapist and his supervisor that he was not to speak with my son again. All the sessions did was make it harder for my son.

Month after month in the hospital with so-called professionals seemed to be making no progress. If I had known then what I know now, I would have been more assertive with the doctors and therapists, asked more questions, maybe even taken him out of the hospital sooner.

Jon was discharged from the hospital in April of 1985, with a recommendation that he follow up with a mental health system in Ohio. When I picked him up to return to Ohio, we stopped for lunch at a local restaurant. He went to the restroom and when he returned to the table he said "Mom, I just threw all my meds down the toilet. I'd rather be crazy than a zombie." I couldn't blame him—nor could I convince him to keep taking the meds. After all, he had been on meds for seven months and they had not helped at all. So we returned to Columbus, where he continued to live like a hermit in the basement, slowly deteriorating

Chapter 8

Schizophrenia is a disease of the brain (a chemical imbalance) which affects the thought process. The symptoms are depression, lack of motivation, sometimes obsession, the lack of personal hygiene, suicide ideation, the hearing of voices, and delusions. Jon had them all. In the beginning of this long, painful journey

I got very frustrated with Jon's lack of motivation, his messy room, his refusal to attend to his personal hygiene. I would try to encourage him, sometimes even nag him. Then someone asked me, "What was Jon like before he became ill?" He was self-motivated, had a paper route, got good grades, was in sports and kept his room neat and clean, was meticulous in terms of his personal hygiene. "Then," she said," His current behavior is due to his illness. You can encourage him, but don't get frustrated. He's doing the best he can." That advice brought me some peace. I began to accept his behavior as part of his illness and no longer tried to figure out how to fix him. I just loved him as he was.

The voices Jon David heard were the most difficult of the symptoms he experienced. In the beginning I tried to rationalize with him, telling him the voices weren't real. As I learned more about mental illness I realized I was wrong. The voices were as real to him as my voice. At first Jon indicated that he enjoyed the voices—they were good company. But it wasn't long before they became harsh, cruel, almost demonic. I remember suggesting he watch TV or listen to music when the voices got too loud. He responded, "No, Mom. You don't understand. The voices talk to me through the TV and music."

It was difficult for him to be in any social setting with the voices always present. He spent a lot of his time pacing back and forth in his room trying somehow to soothe the voices. Nothing worked.

I'll never forget one incident that indicated to me how bad the voices were. Jon was living at home with me at the time. I came home from work one noon, and he said, "Mom the voices told me to eat crap. I tried so hard not to listen to them, but finally I gave up. I went downstairs to the kitty litter box and ate cat crap." As he told me, tears were falling down his face and my heart broke. The mental torment he was in was unimaginable.

Another time I came home and he met me at the door telling me not to come into the house. The voices had told him that there was a gas leak in the house and if I came in it would blow up. I stayed outside until he went through the house checking out everything he could to make sure it was safe.

At times the voices would tell him he should hurt me or his sister because we were conspiring against him. He would tell me this so I could protect us from him as he struggled and fought against these voices.

No medication seemed to calm the voices. There continued to be times when Jon was not med compliant. When the meds seemed not to help and the side effects were bad, he would choose to stop taking the meds. Nothing seemed to help the voices. He lived with them, struggled against them day after day, week after week, month after month, year after year.

There were times when Jon was incessantly preoccupied with a "past life." He believed he had been reincarnated and that in the past life he was some sort of mass murderer. He would speak of himself as "Miller the Killer" (Miller being his last name). Because of this belief, that he had been a serial killer, Jon felt he deserved his mental illness. My gentle, kind son would be the last person in the world to hurt or kill anyone, but while in this delusion nothing could persuade him otherwise.

Chapter 9

In the fall of 1986 Jon and I moved up north to be with my daughter who was spending her senior year in high school living with my parents. As Jon became ill, she responded by running around, not attending class, basically showing self-destructive behavior. She just couldn't handle her big brother's illness. We had been advised by a counselor to get her out of Columbus if she had any chance of graduation. So she moved in with my parents and did very well there.

This move meant separation from my husband. It was a difficult, painful decision for me. Thirty years later I still have occasional nightmares about this. He and I still loved each other, but I found myself in a position of having to choose between my husband and my children. It broke my heart, but I felt I had to do it. He continued to have brain tumors and a few years after I left him he passed away at the young age of forty-five. I knew he understood and accepted my decision, and we continued to keep in touch and love each other. Nevertheless I had to focus on my children.

Over the following years Jon was hospitalized six times, mostly for at least two weeks at a time. I could usually get him to admit himself when his condition deteriorated to a low point. But in January of 1988 his symptoms became worse and he refused to admit himself. I had no choice but to petition the court to force him to be hospitalized.

Fortunately I spoke with a judge who understood that Jon's lack of personal hygiene and extreme depression, his failure to take care of himself, to eat properly, lack of sleep could be viewed as hurting himself—in a sense a slow suicide. Most judges would need proof that he was in imminent danger to himself or others, but this judge saw the bigger picture and ordered Jon to be hospitalized. It was a terrible time. The sheriff came to our house and took Jon out in handcuffs. I cannot put into words how that made me feel. To see my precious son being arrested because of my actions was terrible Even though I knew it was for his own good, his sister Rachel and I were devastated and cried for hours, holding each other as we mourned the devastation that our son, our brother was experiencing.

A week later I had to go to court to testify against him. There he was at the defense table in handcuffs with his court-appointed lawyer. On the other side was I, his mother, along with case workers from the hospital and the mental health system who had been working with Jon. By this time Jon was calm and testified that he was fine, didn't have to be hospitalized. I had to testify to his self-destructive behavior and deterioration. In the end the judge ordered him to be involuntarily hospitalized at in the psychiatric unit of the local hospital for ninety days. Unfortunately, he made little progress during this time.

Chapter 10

In between hospitalizations Jon attended a partial hospitalization program several times a week. This was the hospital's outpatient program for those with chronic mental illness. There he was involved in some group therapy sessions and activities such as arts and crafts. His favorite activity was making moccasins which he wore constantly and was always having to make a new pair when they were worn out. I still have the last pair he made. This program gave him some structure to his week but didn't really help. He eventually stopped going.

During these years he was a client of the local mental health system, a state-funded program for those with developmental disability and mental illness. It was put in place following the deinstitutionalizing of people with mental illness that occurred in the 1970s. They provided a psychiatrist, therapists, case workers, and a number of programs serving the clients and their needs. Many of these professionals were caring individuals, wanting to help their clients. But the continued cut in funding, low salaries, and continued increase in clients made it difficult for this to be an effective program. Case managers and therapists had too many clients and the one psychiatrist could see clients only once every three months. Thirty years later the funding has only decreased and the program has lessened its ability to serve those in the community who need their services.

At this time Jon was involved with a support team provided by the mental health system that served clients wherever they lived. They were supposed to make sure meds were taken, grocery shopping was done, bills were paid, and to engage the client socially. I remember one of these professionals who really cared for Jon and did his best to befriend him and keep him on top of his living/social skills. In my opinion the rest seemed to just be doing their job—and not so well at that.

I was told on a number of occasions that I should let Jon be more independent and was assured that the support team would work with him, making sure he needs were met. But I remember one cold November day I got a call from Jon (he was living in an apartment) asking if he could come home for the weekend. His gas bill hadn't been paid and his skylight was still open. He was freezing. Because the support team had made such a big deal about my "letting Jon go" he was hesitant to call me. He ended up coming home for the weekend, and on Monday I made sure his gas was turned on. As you can imagine, I was furious at the support team and no longer trusted them to make sure Jon's basic needs were met. Certainly I wanted him to be as independent as possible, but he needed support which, clearly, the support team was unable or couldn't be trusted to give him.

Other parents experienced much of what I did in terms of the mental health system. Part of the problem was they felt they were the professionals and seemed to feel that they didn't need to listen to us, the parents. We found it difficult to communicate with them because of this attitude. Yes, they were the experts, especially in terms of medication. But *we*, the parents were experts when it came to our children. Our frustration was that we believed that we should all be working together for the benefit of our children but were seldom listened to.

Chapter 11

Off and on during Jon's journey with mental illness he lived with me. It was often necessary but not an ideal situation for either him or me. It is difficult for an adult to be living with his mother, and it was hard for me to see him on a daily basis deteriorate when I could do nothing to help him. I never knew from day to day what new crisis would occur. Whenever he was discharged from the hospital, it was strongly suggested that he not move back home. While I agreed with them, options were few and far between.

After having Jon live at home for five years into his illness, I finally made the difficult decision during one of his hospital stays that he could not come home to live. It was time for all of us to begin the separation process. He was placed in what we were told was the best adult foster care group home in the county and, indeed, it appeared clean, and the caregivers seemed to be interested in the residents.

I experienced a tremendous relief when Jon moved into the home. For the first time in years the daily burden seemed to be lifted a little. I was so weary--working full time and never knowing what I would come home to. Now I could breathe. I could come home from work and not have to worry that Jon might have hurt himself—or worse--while I was gone. The house was as I left it in the morning, not filled with cigarette smoke and clutter. I could spend an evening reading in peace and quiet rather than listening to Jon talk about his illness and pace the floor in his bedroom. I was grateful that he was in a safe, clean home where he was getting the supervision and care he needed. Financially it was a burden, since I had to supplement his government check to enable him to have some spending money and help him purchase clothes or other items he needed. But the relief and freedom I experienced after five difficult years more than compensated for the additional expense.

As time went on, however, I began to have some concerns. From bits and pieces of conversations with Jon and several other residents, I began to suspect that things were not as good as I had thought. In spite of an estimated income of over $4000 a month, the caregivers were very skimpy with meals for the resident (no seconds, no milk, only peanut butter and jelly sandwiches for lunch), while their family often ate better meals eaten separately from the residents. Residents could smoke only on a screened-in porch which had no chairs and was freezing in the winter, having no storm windows, while the caregivers freely smoked in the house. The residents were not allowed in the kitchen, even to get a cup of coffee.

I began to hear stories of temper tantrums on the part of the caregivers, and it appeared that the residents were often treated like children rather than disabled adults. There were no consistent encouragements or opportunities for socialization, and there were incidents when the residents were instructed to be gone from the house for a period of time so that the caregivers could have parties without their presence.

Another area of concern was the fact that the caregivers had four young children, two of whom slept on the same floor as the residents, with their parents sleeping two floors below with the other two children. Aside from the fact that this was not an appropriate arrangement for the children, it also was unfair for the adult residents to have to share their living space and bathroom with children. It became increasingly clear to me that the individual needs and rights of the residents were not a priority for the caregivers.

Speaking to the mental health system was pointless. Their idea of checking up on the situation was to go over to the house and ask the residents in front of the caregivers if they had any complaints. Not exactly the best way to achieve accurate information! Another aspect of this situation was the fact that if an advocate spoke up and criticized the caregiver directly or by the means of mental health system, it was inevitable that those residing in the home would be made to pay in one way or another. It proved an excellent way of controlling the families—of keeping them from "making waves." Most of the time this was a subtle thing, but the residents were very aware that this was the practice and would rather put up with violation of their rights and neglect of their needs than to live with the results that would occur if they or their families complained. It was very unpleasant to live with people who subtly or overtly ostracize you or make you feel unwelcome.

After nine months of living in this adult foster care home, Jon was given a two-week notice for refusing to comply with his medication as prescribed. (It is quite common among those with mental illness to go through periods when they go off their meds. Sometimes the side effects just become too severe. At other times the person is feeling better so they decide they no longer need the meds.)

This action on the part of the caregivers and my ensuing grievance were my initiation into the fine art of advocacy. The very nature of mental illness robs one's relatives of the ability to defend themselves against such attitudes—of speaking out against the injustices they encounter. And it is my opinion that the "system" understands this well and uses it to their advantage. Medicate them, intimidate them, isolate them. Such an unwritten policy certainly eliminates problems and makes the job of caring for persons with mental illness a lot less trouble.

One night after dropping Jon off at the adult foster care home and watching my precious son walk with head bowed, greasy long hair covering his face, I wrote:

SEE YA LATER

He walks in the cold toward a colder house.
I watch him shuffling slowly, head bent,
His long disheveled hair covering his face.
The car's warmth suffocates me.

"Why, God?" I cry and slam
My hands against the steering wheel.
Snow covers the windows, leaves me hidden
On the side of the road. Alone, angry
I battle in the dark with a shadow god
Who doesn't hear my curses or my prayers.

The windshield wipers let some light
Into my dark and hidden space,
Their sound momentarily soothing
My weary soul. But the car is cold now.
I won't be traveling far enough for it to get warm.

Chapter 12

When Jon left the adult foster care home, I was encouraged not to allow him back into my house. The only option at the time was the city mission, so I dropped him off with his suitcase and left. The next morning he came walking home carrying his suitcase—empty. Overnight someone had stolen all the items that had been in his suitcase. So here he was again…at home with no other options.

In the summer of 1990 the support team found Jon and his friend an apartment over one of the downtown stores. It was a crummy place, with windows that didn't open, a skylight that didn't close, cracked linoleum, stained rugs. But Jon was happy to move in, and the support team assured me that they would support the two of them. Jon's roommate was a beer drinker, and soon Jon joined him. They would sit around all day and night drinking, with no accountability on the part of the support team.

Drinking is especially harmful since alcohol affects the same part of the brain as the psychiatric medication which neutralizes the benefits of the meds. Over the months bills weren't paid, food was scarce, and often Jon spent days alone since his roommate spent time with other friends outside the apartment. I tried to stay out of things (as requested by the support team, but found that there was little support for Jon by the support team no matter how often I met with them to discuss the situation. I'm his mother. How could I let him suffer as once again the "system" was failing him?

Chapter 13

During this time I began to hear that a new medication (clozaril) was approved by the FDA and being used with success for people with schizophrenia. It was being viewed as the first breakthrough in many years, and I had hope for the first time in years that Jon could be helped.

Normally Jon went to his psychiatrist appointment (a fifteen minute appointment every three months) on his own. He told me he just went in and said what he needed to say to get out of the appointment as soon as possible. He felt, with good reason, that no one in the mental health system really listened to him and, if they did, pretty much made him feel he didn't know what he was talking about.

With this new information about clozaril, I called and insisted on making an appointment as soon as possible to speak with the psychiatrist. When Jon and I entered the doctor's office, it was clear he was not happy that I was there. I will never forget what ensued.

When I asked the doctor if he would prescribe this new medication for Jon he replied, "That's only for people who are really sick. Jon doesn't need it." My response was, "Jon hears voices all the time, he's depressed, he's talking about suicide. And you don't think he's sick enough to try this new medication? Clearly what he's on isn't helping." Yet the doctor refused.

Chapter 14

Throughout Jon's painful, lonely journey his "comforter-in-chief" was Frieda, our family dog. When Jon was about eight years old his stepfather brought home a puppy we named Frieda. Once she was past the puppy chew-everything-up stage, she was a wonderful friend, a real member of our family. When we moved to Holland we took her with us.

When Jon lived with me, he stayed in his bedroom upstairs much of the time. Frieda spent most of her time up there with him. It's amazing how animals sense pain in their owners and are there for them. Many a day I would walk upstairs and find them curled up together, either sleeping or Jon petting Frieda and she giving him "kisses" on his face. She was Jon's friend when others couldn't be.

One winter weekend I chaperoned with my teacher friend a group of high school girls on a skiing trip. It was an enjoyable time, a relief from the day-to-day roller coaster ride on my journey with Jon. But when I got home reality hit me in the face. My sister and Rachel had had to put Jon in the hospital again. At the same time Frieda had become suddenly ill and they took her to the vet who advised putting her down. They were just waiting until I got home.

I found myself struggling with what to do in this situation. Should I just have her put down without Jon knowing it, or should I try to give him a chance to say good-by to his friend. I talked to the hospital therapist and decided it was important for Jon to know what was going on. I spoke with him, and he decided he wanted to see Frieda again before she died. The doctor gave Jon an hour's pass and we went to the vet's to say good-by to our dear friend. Rachel, Jon and I kissed her and hugged her with tears streaming down our faces. Then I held her while she received the shot which ended her life. Jon was so medicated that I still am not sure how important it was for him to be there. But I'm glad I made that decision

Chapter 15

In November of 1990 we opened our first Ladder Home. I convinced Jon to move there where I knew he would get support and live in a quality, affordable, appropriate home. Since I was co-founder I did my best to stay out of Jon's business and let the house managers support him. Unfortunately by this time Jon's illness was so severe that nothing much could be done for him. No medication alleviated his voices/delusions. It seemed that all hope was gone

On Easter Day 1991 Jon and I joined the family at my parent's house to celebrate. Jon stayed for only an hour or so and then asked me to take him home. In the car he said, "I really want to be with my family, but it's so depressing to be around my cousins who seem to be happy and successful while I'm just stuck. If things don't change in the next month or so, I'm going to take my life by shooting myself." This was not an unusual statement for him. He often indicated similar thoughts.

Several weeks later Jon admitted himself to the hospital on his own without my assistance (or insistence). For the first time since the onset of his illness he had decided to work with the doctors in terms of his medication, believing that the haldol needed to be increased. I was encouraged and felt that this might be a turn for the better.

I was surprised when, on April 29, 1991 I received a call from one of the support team members, stating that the hospital psychiatrist had requested a meeting with me, the support team, and the mental health system psychiatrist. I indicated that at the time I had not planned to request a meeting, but if the psychiatrist thought it necessary, I would make arrangements to get off work. The meeting was to be held at 9:30 on Tuesday, April 30.

While I had never met the hospital psychiatrist prior to this meeting, I had heard about him from members of the local NAMI (National Alliance for the Mentally Ill) support group. He had spoken to the group earlier in the year and had infuriated them with his outspoken criticism of family involvement in the treatment of persons with mental illness. Regardless of this, I was impressed that he had chosen to call a "team meeting" regarding Jon and went into the meeting determined to do my best to keep an open mind. I believe that I approached the meeting with a cooperative attitude, as I had done throughout my involvement with both the mental health system and the hospital. I had no reason to expect anything less from the other participants in this meeting.

Initially the hospital psychiatrist addressed the issue of Jon's medication. He had decided (over Jon's protest) that Jon was not capable of consistent oral med compliance and would be starting him on monthly injections. Jon did have a history of this, although the whole point of admitting himself to the hospital at this time was based on his recognition of needing *more* medication.

Jon had come a long way in the previous six months in accepting his mental illness. While I was a little disturbed at the doctor's rather arrogant and inflexible attitude, I nevertheless simply asked several questions about side effects of the meds and the length of time it should take for the meds to take effect. The psychiatrist then asked me what I thought to be a strange question. He said, "Are you comfortable with the mental health system psychiatrist and Jon dealing with his meds?" I couldn't understand why the question was asked, but answered, "If Jon is comfortable, so am I." Jon just sat there in silence.

Then the attack on me began. The hospital psychiatrist brought up the issue of Jon's living in the Ladder House. He said, "Jon doesn't need the structure and rules and regulations of the Ladder house. He is perfectly capable of independent living. Your involvement in the house is a problem for Jon."

When I began to question the basis for his opinion, especially since he admitted he didn't know much about the Ladder program, he brought the rest of the "team" into the conversation to substantiate his claims. From then on the conversation deteriorated into an argument for over an hour, with the team questioning my involvement in Jon's life and my defending both that involvement and the Ladder House.

The hospital psychiatrist remained in control of the meeting, treating me *in front of my son* in an arrogant and condescending way. I was told that my involvement in the house was allowing Jon to get away with breaking the rules, that I was too involved in

Jon's life, and that I could not be both a mother and an advocate. They said, "Every time you get involved in advocacy it makes it awkward for Jon." This was denied by Jon, which they ignored. It was also denied by me, which they refused to accept.

I finally just shut up, tears falling down my cheeks. (When I am really angry my response is usually crying instead of shouting.) Clearly I was upset as was Jon. He had admitted himself to the hospital because of suicide ideation and desire to get help and a day later he was subjected to watching his mother being harassed by the very people who were supposed to be helping him. In addition, his own opinions on meds and on the issues brought up were ignored.

Finally Jon stood and said, "Come on, Mom. We're getting out of here." He took my hand and led me out of the room. Jon spent one more night in the hospital and then, against the doctor's recommendation, signed himself out. Any trust he had in the hospital or mental health system was gone. He wanted nothing more to do with any of them. He had, in effect, lost any little bit of hope he had that things could get better.

I hugged my son and told him I would pick him up in the morning and take him back to his room at Ladder. I tried to keep it together in front of him. But when I got to my car I closed the door and just lost it. Once again the "system" had failed my son. Once again they thought they knew what was best for him without listening to him (or me) and at least taking our opinion into consideration.

I was so angry. We were treated with such disrespect. After years of fighting for my son, of trying to work with the "professionals" to help my son, I, too, felt helpless, hopeless. My anger and frustration and my deep love for Jon David engulfed me and screams poured out of me as I slumped in my car. My anger and pain pushed out the tears that had so often been held inside as year after year I fought for my son. Now what?

As I've said before, if I had known what I know now I would have fought harder against the system. I would have refused to accept the passivity and negligence of those who were required/paid to help my son, but too often let him fall through the cracks. I would have been much more of a "mama grizzly."

Would it have changed anything? I don't know. That is my regret. However, I have come to peace with my failures. I know I did the best I could with what I knew at the time. And I know I loved him unconditionally and would have given my life for him.

Chapter 16

It was early in the morning of June 6. 1991. I was working in the office of the theatre department at the local college. People were coming in and going out of my office getting ready for a busy day. Suddenly one of the faculty members came in and put his hand on my shoulder. He asked me to come with him to my boss' office. Because I was known as something of the counselor/pastor of the department, I assumed that one of the company members or staff was in need of my help.

As I walked into the office I saw two strangers dressed in suits with somber looks on their faces. They asked me, "Are you Jon

Miller's mother?" I knew instantly what they were going to tell me. My first question was, "Did he kill himself or was he killed?" Strangely I was relieved when they responded that he had taken his own life. My feeling was that he had made the decision about his own life—he took charge in a way he hadn't been able to do for years. Then my heart stopped, I slumped in a chair, and the tears flowed. My precious son was gone. The threats he had made for years had become a reality. Our journey together was over. My heart expanded with a huge hole never to be filled.

"Is there someone you can call?" I was asked. I called my brother whom I knew would be my strength for what lay ahead. He came to the office immediately. When we got to the car he put his head down on the steering wheel and wept like a baby. I had never seen my brother cry before. Ours were the first of many tears to be shed in the coming hours, weeks, months, and, indeed, years.

The worst thing I now had to do was to tell Jon's sister, his aunt and his grandparents. We found Rachel (his sister) at her boyfriend's house. As soon as she saw me she cried out "Jon?" "Yes," I said as I walked to her, my arms open. She fell to the ground and wailed.

It was a terrible/beautiful sound. I wish I could have responded that way—I did inside. But I had to hold it together for my family and for all the decisions I would have to make in the days to come. My wailing took place when I was alone in bed, grieving both the life and death of my son. Several of my friends didn't want me to be alone and offered to spend the night with me. But I wanted, I needed, to be alone that first night without my son. I lay in bed and cried myself to sleep. It would be the first of many such nights.

The next morning my brother and I went to the funeral home to make the arrangements for Jon's funeral and burial. One of the things they asked me to bring was a picture of Jon so they could use it to make sure he looked as best as they could make him. I took his high school senior picture. Jon had shot himself in the chest, so I knew his face would be easy for them to "makeup." The next morning they called me and said, "I think you should come down and look at Jon before the viewing." They thought maybe I would prefer to have a closed casket. With trepidation I went, scared at what I would see. I had never seen a dead body, much less the body of my son. They took me into the room and I looked down at my son.

I began crying uncontrollably. He looked so wonderful! They had cut his hair to match his high school picture, the frowns that always covered his face were gone. He looked so peaceful for the first time in years. My beautiful, beautiful son—dead, but at peace.

During a family conversation regarding what I was going to say at Jon's funeral, my young nephew said under his breath, "He was a good son and he died." Leave it to a child to get to the very essence of reality.

At his funeral, the pastor referred to God's word, "'Come to me all ye who are weary and heavy laden, I will give you rest.' Jon's spirit cried out for the way out. Sometimes his spirit was clouded. It was rest, peace that Jon David sought and struggled for. All of us cry out for the comfort that only God can give us. Jon David found a resolution to his struggle and was welcomed by God. The same God who said to Jon David '...I will give you rest' will give you and me who are left behind that same rest."

Chapter 17

When the pastor was through I spoke. As hard as it was I felt compelled to speak for my son since he could no longer speak for himself. "Those of us who knew and loved Jon David mourn his separation from us. He was truly a good son, a good brother, a good friend. We miss his shy smile, his sense of humor, his gentle, sweet spirit which was always present even in the midst of his pain and torment."

"Jon David fought the voices for years. In life, nothing he did brought him relief. The last act was the act of a victor, not a victim. It was his choice, not our choice. Searching the depths of his heart for the truth, for the way out, it was rest/peace that Jon longed for, that he struggled for. He has now found a resolution to the struggle in his life. His final act which was carefully planned and carried out was the choice of a man who survived in this world only because of incredible courage."

"Jon was, indeed, a good son. He fought until he could fight no more. His choice was not one which I would have made for him, but it was *his* choice—apparently the only one he thought he had. He was brave and good and worthy of much more than life offered him. My prayer is that his death will somehow make a difference to others who, like him, are victims of a cruel disease and a society that too often fails to listen and respond to persons in pain."

Chapter 18

> *Years and years of torment. Making deadlines for*
> *when he would take his life. Horrified when those*
> *days came. They would pass. Until June 6, 1991.*
>
> -Rachel's Voice

Growing up, Jon was a son to be proud of. He was an excellent student, a responsible boy and young man who was very popular among his peers. His overriding passion was music. A brilliant percussionist, he won many awards during his high school years and was never so happy as when he was "pounding on his drums." A member of his high school marching band, jazz ensemble, and orchestra, as well as several rock groups, Jon's dream was to play professionally. That dream was cut short by the onset of schizophrenia during his junior year of high school.

The day before his death he came to my house and spent hours down in the basement playing his drums. I remember saying to his sister Rachel, "I've never heard him playing with such passion and skill." He knew it would be the last time. After that his drums fell silent.

During the writing of Jon David's story for feedback I sent several drafts to my brother who has a background in advertising and publishing. In one of the last calls I got from him he spoke gently, directly to me. "Through much of this I hear a reporter relaying this story. I want to hear more of a grieving mother," he said. After a few seconds I responded, "Maybe I now need to be that grieving mother."

After that conversation, I spent a period of time away from my keyboard processing his suggestion and my response. I trust my brother and accepted his thoughts as true. But where did my response come from? I've been a grieving mother for over twenty years Why wasn't that coming through in my writing?

A year after Jon died we planted rose bushes at the Ladder House, in my yard, and his grandparents' yard. After all these years they still bloom. Every year I watch the rose bush. And every year the first rose blooms no sooner and no later, but exactly on June 6. Jon is still with me. In response to this, I wrote the following in memory of Jon David:

I WILL REMEMBER YOU

I will remember you
When the roses bloom.
The thorns, though necessary,
Are insignificant when measured against
The beauty and fragrance of the flower.

I will remember you
When the roses bloom.
Life's thorns multiplied
And threatened to kill the rose
That was you. But your gentle, stubborn spirit
Would not accept this death-life,
And chose to become a forever rose.

I will remember you
When the roses bloom.

The thorns on the branches, your pain;
The dew on the petals, your tears;
The unfolding bud, the promise of beauty that
Was not to be realized in this life;
The rose in bloom, the spirit that now is you.

So, I return to the earth in memory of you, Jon David,
The rose.
Your fragrance and beauty live on
In the planning and blooming of each bush.
And your sweet, gentle spirit lives on for eternity,
Planted firmly in the hearts of those who love you so.

I will remember you
When the roses bloom.

Do I miss my son? Of course I do. In fact, strangely, I love him more now that he is dead. I wonder why? When I see him in my mind's eye as a toddler my heart breaks. Why is it so hard to look at pictures of him as a little boy? Looking at a photograph of him all dressed up for his first (and last) prom I mourn for his dreams/my dreams of a life that was never to be. The first parade I attended following Jon's death found me sobbing as the percussion division marched by, and I heard those drums playing. It took me by surprise. I just didn't expect such pain. Even now the tears still come. That should be *my* son playing the cymbals or beating on the bass drum or playing the snare drums. That *was* my son before his mental illness took over.

I dream of him often. The other night the dream was so real...he was so real...that I woke up wailing, wanting to hold him once more. Do I wish he would be back here with me? Selfishly, yes. But not if it means that he would still be living in the torment he experienced as he fought the voices, the delusions, the depression. In the last few years of his life he often told me that what he wanted was peace. It never came in life. On his gravestone is written: "You have found your peace, now rest. "That says it all for me.

Indeed, his drums are now silent. I kept his drum set in my basement for more than twenty years following his death, in part to keep him with me and also with the thought that one day one of my grandchildren might follow in his footsteps. That did not happen. A year ago my daughter came to me and said she had a friend who was starting a band and needed a drum set. She and I agreed that it was time...that Jon would want his drums to come alive again. So the drums are gone, as silent as they have been for over twenty years. But I still hear them in my memory.

His drums fell silent,
The voices still speak.
In death he found victory,
In God he found peace.

Augustine wrote, "The tears...streamed down, and I let them flow freely as they would, making them a pillow for my heart. On them I rest." So it is for me after all these years and will be until I am with him once again.

My grief is a long journey. It will never end. Oh, the deep pain subsides with time. I find myself embracing the loss I carry each day. But then for some reason or for no reason, grief shatters my comfortable journey and hits me with all its power. I find myself curled up in my bed or on the floor holding and rocking myself trying to find comfort, relief. It ebbs and flows in unpredictable ways I do not understand but have come to accept.

My grief is a lonely journey. Following Jon's death, I was surrounded with family and friends trying to comfort and support me. Throughout the past 22 years I have been and still am blessed to be surrounded with family and friends. Still, I am alone in my pain and grief, unable to be truly comforted or understood by any of them. In my bedroom on my bed of grief and rest, I find myself overwhelmed by my loss. It is there I discover that comfort and peace emanate from my God alone who lies on my bed with me, holding me in strong, loving arms, whispering that he understands, that he too lost a son. I feel his healing tears falling on my cheek, and I rest.

I began grieving Jon long before his death. Jon's illness took him down a dark path I could not follow. There were times when I was horrified at my thought, "I wish he would die for himself but also for me."

The Jon I knew...his dreams, his personality that was so vibrant, that toddler in a white sailor's hat observing ants...was fading. I was losing him to some dark and terrifying illness that couldn't be cured. I saw no future but continued torment and destruction. And he felt the same way as he continued to have suicidal ideation. Yes, a part of me wished he would die in order to bring peace to him…and, yes, to me.

So on that day that Jon David took his life I was not shocked. I had suspected it was coming for years. I had grieved him for years. So the mourning on that day was an extension of my former grief. But now he was really gone. There was no longer that sliver of hope that some miracle would bring him back to me. He was just gone.

Two weeks after Jon died I returned to my daily routine. I was working forty hours a week, attending seminary, working with the newly-formed Ladder Homes, and trying to be a mom to my daughter Rachel. Grief was intermittent. I just didn't have/take the time to allow myself the luxury, if you will, to truly mourn the loss of my son. Life went on. And I did what I had to do to survive.

Now, all these years later, I am retired, Ladder Homes is doing well, and I am writing this story. I have time to grieve deeply and my brother's comment has given me this gift. I take out the old pictures and weep over all of them. I listen to Larnelle Harris' "I Have Friends in High Places" and know with a combination of grief and joy that one day I will see my son again, that, in fact, he is with me now. I mourn with every hymn I sing and sermon I hear in church. I spent an hour with my pastor a few weeks ago crying out for my son, for the journey that is now over. I have rewritten portions of this story as I dig deeper into my memories and feelings.

Everyone grieves differently, it is true. Mine is now in full bloom and the healing it brings is so bitter-sweet. I am now a grieving mother and will be until I die. Can you tell?

RACHEL'S VOICE (JON DAVID'S SISTER)

Remembering my brother, Jon David Miller, is a mixed bag of emotions. The memories of our childhood—so much fun, playing music with him and recording ourselves on tape cassettes, and rewinding them over and over and just belly laughing. The memories of him on the drum line and me on the dance team and the lights on in the stadium—knowing we were both out there together. Then there was his election to the homecoming court, and because of that my mother escorted him onto the field, so there we were, all of us under the lights. I have no better memory than that night. It was an overwhelming feeling of joy.

Of course there were the times that we grooved to Michael Jackson and the rock band Kiss. One hour of his practice everyday after school. I went crazy most of the time, but he was so good and would listen to a number of genres of music. I learned about jazz, blues, rock, rhythm and blues and Motown. Musical education I would use later in life and would always thank Jon for teaching me those things.

Jon David was such a sweet brother and young man. Everybody in school had such respect for him. He was extremely talented and yet so humble. He had the nicest girlfriend and of course those girls who had crushes on him and always tried to get to him through me. I knew better. He was a one-woman man. He was so in love.

Jon David and I also had three step brothers. For the moste part we all got along, but there were also times when that dynamic would play a role in the family and we became a dysfunctional family. With both of our sensitive spirits, there were times we just couldn't take the chaos. I had temper tantrums and screamed and yelled and fought one of the boys it seems everyday. Never Jon David though.

Then the darkness came in. Oh how I couldn't take what was happening to my big brother. "What was going on," I would say to my mom constantly. Night after night of him screaming and throwing himself around in his bedroom. What was this horror? Whenever I could I would run away from home. My grades started suffering. I was in an unhealthy relationship with a boy who lived way on the other side of Columbus, Ohio. At times, stealing the car from my parents just to escape all the noise. My step father got his first brain tumor when I was in the 8th grade. It was not malignant, but it disabled him. During the next twelve years he had seven of them and let the last one take his life. At this time one of my step brothers was still living with us and started smoking marijuana. We all just couldn't take the stress of the illness of our dad and the fast decline of Jon David's health.

Mom took him to all kinds of doctors. I just remember him putting a towel over his head over a pan of boiling wawter constantly. He constantly was reading the Bible and quoting scriptures and giving count downs to the day that he would decide to give up. There was a horrible incident with my step father and Jon David actually thought he killed him. I just saw so much blood and my brother ran out the front door, and I ran out of the back door, screaming in terror. Things just continued to rapidly decline. He broke up with his girlfriend and continued to isolate himself. We spent a lot of time watching movies still whenever I was home. He thought my boyfriend was cool and never ever judged me. There were a few moments that he thought I was doing something stupid, and would say so. I hung as close to him as I could.

Then there came the time for me to leave my life in Columbus. Leave Jon David, leave my mom and leave all of my friends without even saying goodbye to them. I had to. It was so chaotic in my home that a Christian counselor suggested that if I had somewhere else to live, I should consider it. Three days later I was packed up and Mom drove me up to Holland MI where my grandparents lived. Shortly thereafter she went back to Columbus to attend to Jon David and my step father. A time that was a grueling process and frustrating time for my mother, as she decided to finally leave my step father after many attempts to save the marriage. She brought my brother up to Holland and we were all together again. A major change culturally, physically, spiritually and psychologically. Shock!!

In and out of mental health wards. Trying so hard to ease the mental pain. "What can I do?" Jon would say. "These voices just won't stop." Hating to see the pain that he was in and the torment of the voices telling him what to do and the attempts to cut himself were too much for me. I ran. I managed to continue college, but never came home until very late in the morning.

I tried to make contact with my biological father. Made contact. Next day the number was disconnected. "Why? My brother needed you. My mother needed your support. How could you?" Jon David spent all of his time listening to music and smoking cigarettes constantly. He didn't want the medication. "It makes me feel like a zombie, Rach." "I know, Jon, but if it quiets the voices, why won't you take them?" I screamed on the inside. I was so angry with him that he wouldn't try to help himself. What could I do or say to help him. (absolutely helpless). I ran away over and over. Just couldn't see it. He actually did not bathe for almost a year. Mom had to force him to get help. I can't imagine how she felt. We thought it was for his own good.

Years and years of torment. Making deadlines for when he would take his life. Horrified when those days came. They would pass.

Until June 6, 1991. I approached my boyfriend's home after work. I saw all these cars around his home. I recognized them. Why were they there? My heart dropped to the pit of my stomach. I walked in the door and there they all were. My mom reached out to me and said, "Jon David." I dropped my books and took off, running and screaming in a pain that I never knew existed. I collapsed. Total shock. "He is okay," said one of the voices. "You mean he is okay; he just hurt himself bad and is in the hospital. You mean he is really okay?" Hoping, pleading for the answer I wanted. No. It never came. He was truly gone. Some hikers found him in some woods lying by Black River here in Holland. All the attempts of cutting on himself, all of the dates of promising to "end it." It was here. He shot himself in the heart. No turning back once he made that choice. My big brother, my only sibling, my place to go to for advice, which was very ironic now that I look back on it. He was GONE FOREVER!!! No more. No more words, no more laughter and silliness, no more making fun of mom, no more, nothing. Complete silence.

The drums were silent. He played them the last time I was in his presence a couple days before. Playing like never before. Long and beautiful. He even brought over friends to hear him. In his glory. Did he know? Had he made his decision already? Oh, my precious brother. I miss you dearly. I share stories with my children, Hasia and Jaren. I ache for them that they never got to know their Uncle Jon. They sure know how silly you were. I ache for you. I know you found your peace, but twenty two years later I have more pain, but somehow I have peace. Mixed emotions. Bittersweet memories. Please come to me. Please come back to me.

The Jon David Miller Home

Ladder 3

Ladder 4

Part III

God's Voice (Ladder Homes)

I was hungry and you fed me,
I was thirsty and you gave me a drink,
I was homeless and you gave me a room,
I was shivering and you gave me clothes,
I was sick and you stopped to visit,
I was in prison and you came to me.
I'm telling you the solemn truth: Whenever you
did one of these things to someone overlooked
or ignored, that was me—you did it to me.
-Matthew 25:36-40

It was February of 1990. In the middle of my journey with Jon David in his struggle with mental illness, I was attending a monthly meeting of NAMI (National Alliance for the Mentally Ill)—a support group for parents of adult children with mental illness. This was a time and place of safety and encouragement, a time to share our sorrows and joys, our frustrations and discouragement, our weariness that comes from journeying with our children as they struggle with their mental illness—bipolar, depression, schizophrenia.

One of the frequent discussions was the lack of appropriate, safe, affordable housing for our children. Some lived in adult foster care homes, which allowed for no privacy and monitored every aspect of their lives, or psychiatric hospitals for periods of time. Others lived in poor, expensive, often unsafe apartments with no support. Some were homeless, living in the city mission, on a friend's couch, even in jail. (I heard on a TV special the other night that there are so many persons with mental illness in jail that jail has become the old mental hospitals.) And in between all these they would often end up home with their family, which was not a good situation for either the family or the adult child. Jon David lived in all of the above except jail.

At this particular NAMI meeting, we had invited as a speaker the Executive Director of H.O.M.E. (Housing Opportunities Made Equitable), a local non-profit housing agency whose mission was to provide affordable housing in our community. We shared with her our frustrations and concerns. Finally she looked us in the eye and said, "Well, what are you going to do about it?" That question was the seed which eventually blossomed into Ladder Homes. After catching our breath, we organized an ad hoc committee on housing (which later incorporated as Ladder Homes) and began to dream of the possibility that we *could* do something about it. We were challenged to "think big" and to consider the possibility of working with H.O.M.E. in acquiring an initial house.

> *All of us need a place*
> *Of our own*
> *A place where we can be alone*
> *Away from everyone else*
> *With ourselves*
> *To do our own*
> *Special thing.*

And so we dreamed.

According to the National Institute of Mental Health (NIMH) it is estimated that there are close to sixty million persons in the United States who have chronic mental illness. One in four Americans suffers from some form of mental illness in their lifetime. If you add to that their families and friends, a significant segment of our fellow Americans is affected by mental illness. In 2004 90% of people who committed suicide had mental illness.

Housing is one of the main challenges for these people. It is estimated that 39% of those homeless are mentally ill. 16% of those incarcerated have undiagnosed or diagnosed mental illness with little or no treatment available. There are three times the number of the mentally ill in prison than in psychiatric hospitals. In Ottawa County (my county) alone there are over one thousand persons with mental illness—and that does not include those who are undiagnosed or being treated by private psychiatrists. Housing programs like Ladder can provide quality, appropriate, affordable housing with case management support for many of them, especially with new medications that allow people with mental illness to live more independently.

H.O.M.E. had just been given a small building which had housed the offices of Holland Ladder and Manufacturing (thus Ladder Homes). Working with H.O.M.E. and volunteer architects and contractors, the committee came up with a plan for remodeling the house to fit the needs of our targeted residents— people who did not need the 24-hour care of adult foster care homes, but were lacking the confidence and living skills (as well as financial means) to live totally independently. This type of home was viewed as a means to fill the housing gap for people with mental illness in our community.

Now we needed to incorporate as a non-profit agency with the State of Michigan, write our by-laws and apply for our non-profit 506(c)(3)status with the federal government, separate from our NAMI chapter for several reasons. First of all, it would focus us solely on housing and, for public awareness, should be seen as such.

Secondly, NAMI is allowed to engage in political activity and advocacy, while a 506(c)(3) tax deductible organization agency is not. Ladder Homes needed to be able to fundraise. NAMI needed to continue to advocate and be politically active. Several of our members (including a lawyer who was on our first Board of Directors) took on this time-consuming project, and we were finally successful in receiving the 506(c)(3) status. Until we received this non-profit status, we worked as an offshoot of H.O.M.E. and the house began to take shape.

We had to tear the house down to its studs, and what a project that was! Many volunteers gathered after work and, under the guidance of a contractor, tore that place apart. The worst part of the refurbishing was taking out the asbestos that had been used as insulation. I can still see that pink nasty stuff being hauled out of the attic. Not an easy job but necessary.

The name we chose for our organization "Ladder Homes" comes from the house we were given by Holland Ladder and Manufacturing. As we were refurbishing the house, we always referred to it as the Ladder house. In addition we saw the house/ our program as "Steps to Independent Living," thus, a ladder to climb up to independent living. It turns out that many of our residents do not go into totally independent living but see Ladder as their permanent home.

While none of us were experts in the building trade or the law, we *were* experts in what our children needed to be as successful and independent as possible. So we came up with the following commitments to our future residents:

- Quality housing (plus furnishings for group home)
- Grounds keeping and building maintenance
- Safe neighborhood
- Available public transportation
- Private bedrooms
- Shared living space
- Rent subsidy to assure affordable housing
- Phone, cable, washer/dryer provided for Ladder 1
- Cleaning supplies for Ladder 1
- Laundry room for both Ladder 1 and each apartment complex
- Residents encouraged to "own" house
- Friendship support from Ladder staff, peers, Community Mental Health, churches, other agencies
- Life and social skills encouraged/taught.
- Regular house meetings held to give residents the opportunity to discuss and resolve household issues
- Chores done by residents with some support
- Ability of residents to monitor own medication and get around community on their own.

- Alcohol or illegal drugs not allowed. Smoking allowed in private bedrooms. (We later changed this to no smoking in the house or apartment.)

Refurbishing the house demanded a volunteer architect, contractor, and 119 volunteers working a total 1,633 hours. In several events we raised $9,542. Fifty one individuals gave furnishings for the house, and 22 churches were involved. This community effort not only allowed us to keep the cost of the house to a minimum but also provided community awareness and excitement about this grass-roots project and Ladder Homes itself.

The small house that we were given was moved to a larger lot, and the refurbishing began. In the midst of the project we needed, of course, to get permits from the city. The city responded to our requests by indicating that we would need a waiver to build a group home in a residential setting.

There was a city meeting where neighbors were invited to speak to our request for a waiver. One woman stood up and said "not in my back yard" and proceeded to tell about a friend of a friend who was chased by a "crazy" person with an axe. Several other neighbors also responded negatively. However, the room was full of our supporters who spoke positively about our project. After this meeting one volunteer began to research the decision by the city to require a waiver. Working with an attorney, she discovered that according to the American Housing. Act, any home for people with disabilities was to be considered a residential home subject only to the regulations for any other home in the neighborhood. In other words, if there is a city regulation that only

10 people could live together in a home, the same would apply to a home for people with disabilities. They are to be considered a family. We presented this information to the city who ended up having to apologize to us and rescind their requirement for a waiver. A victory! We broke that barrier for all the group homes to come in our city.

MISSION AND GOALS

The goals of the Ladder Homes program are:

1. To provide housing that is:
   a. Quality
   b. Affordable
   c. Appropiate
   d. Safe
2. To provide iindividualized seervices for residents that support:
   a. Life and social skills
   b. Integration into the community
   c. Psychiatric stability
   d. Coordination with health professionals and government agencies onan overall treatment plan

The specific target population for residents of Ladder Homes is people with chronic mental illness who are able to function independently with minimal support. None of our homes is licensed or provides 24-hour care, but is privately owned and operated, with Ladder Homes serving as the landlord. We believe that, given the nature of mental illness, homes with all levels of care must be available to provide appropriate, affordable living regardless of the level of care needed.

HOMES

Ladder 1 (later to be renamed the Jon David Miller Home after my son Jon) was opened in November of 1990 to a full house of eight residents and a couple serving as resident assistants. Four women shared the top level of the house, with one full shared bath and a private room for each resident. Four men shared the lower level, again including a shared bath and private rooms. The main floor consisted of a large living area, dining room, kitchen, and half bath. In addition the resident assistants had a suite off the living room with a bedroom, a full bath, and a sitting room.

Our intention for Ladder 1 was to provide housing and support for people with chronic mental illness who can be successful in a supportive living environment. While some changes have been made since 1990 to improve operations, our basic philosophy remains the same. We are firmly committed to providing a private room (or apartment) for each resident, to keep the rent, utilities and housing services to about 35% of the resident's total income, and to continue to, wherever and whenever possible, use volunteers and community services for additional support.

All of this has been a grass-roots project, one which was conceived, planned, and operated totally by families of adult children with mental illness. From start to finish, this was based on our personal knowledge of the needs of our children and other residents.

In May of 1992 we purchased a second house (Ladder 2) for four male residents. Again, each resident had his own private bedroom and a shared living space. We had determined, based on our experience with the residents of Ladder 1, that it was not necessary to have live-in assistants as long as frequent visits by a case worker were provided.

A third house was purchased in 1993 for women. Again, each resident had a private bedroom with shared living space. And, again, case management support was provided on a regular and as needed basis.

After a few years it became clear to the Board that these two 4-bedroom homes (Ladder 2 and 3) were becoming increasingly cost prohibitive. The rent paid (35% of client income) barely covered the mortgage, much less utilities, maintenance, and case management support. So the decision was made to research other options.

In 1996 we sold the two homes and purchased a four-plex apartment unit (each unit had 2 bedrooms). At the time there were enough bedrooms in the group home to move the men from Ladder 2 to Ladder 1. The new apartment facility (Ladder 4) was intended to house women and/or single mothers with children.

In 2001 Ladder 3 was purchased (another four-plex apartment building with two bedrooms per apartment) which has been used for women, single women with children, and married couples.

The rent is subsidized for the apartments at a flat rate per unit, utilities are included in the rent (except cable and phone), and case management support is provided.

After a few years it became apparent that, while the 10 men in Ladder 1 for the most part got along fine, there continued to be issues with having two women sharing an apartment. Differences in terms of keeping the shared areas clean, sleeping hours, and just basic personality clashes created time-consuming case management support and what seemed to be constant chaos and drama in one apartment or another. The Board made the decision to place one woman per apartment, raising the rent slightly. Although clearly the Board took a financial hit and we were able to serve fewer residents, the increased stability for the residents and the lessening of case management time has been worth the cost.

Our dream is to someday have the resources to provide one-bedroom apartments for both men and women, along with the two-bedroom apartments for married couples and single women with children. As previously stated, our group home for men seems to work out well. There are few inter-personal issues, as we empower them to problem-solve among themselves. And, amazingly, the home is kept neat and clean by the men. We do recognize, however, that there are men who at some point would prefer their own apartment and, indeed, would do better in an apartment.

At the current time Ladder Homes is able to provide housing and services for twenty residents. In addition we have what we call our Outreach Program, which provides minimal case management support for five to seven former Ladder residents who have moved on to total independent living or to a more appropriate housing situation. Our motto is "Once a member of the Ladder family, always a member of the Ladder family."

OPERATIONS...RULES/REGULATIONS

Because Ladder Homes are for those people who are able to live independently with minimal support, our philosophy is to have as few regulations as possible.

All our residents must be under the care of a psychologist or doctor and must be able (and willing) to take their own meds and follow their treatment plan as prescribed by their doctor. They must be able to live cooperatively with others and to work on their own or with Ladder staff to resolve problems. Each resident is assured of the quiet enjoyment of the home, and all residents must be willing to cooperate in this regard. Smoking is not allowed in any of the Ladder facilities, nor is alcohol. We do not "police" our residents, so if they choose to drink outside the home and do not come home drunk and disturb others, we have no regulations regarding that. We do, however, encourage residents not to drink or use illegal drugs, mostly because these can interfere with the psychotropic drugs they are taking for their mental illness.

Judyth Thomas

From time to time situations come up which necessitate resolving problems by adding or amending house rules. For instance, at one point a resident (in the group home) was having a female guest over, spending time in his bedroom, which made the other residents uncomfortable. Working with all the residents, it was decided that bedroom doors needed to stay open when a guest was present and that there needed to be a time limit as to when a guest must leave the premises. Another time a resident was allowing a guest to use the laundry facilities and we needed to remind the resident that this laundry facility was designated for residents only. In most cases these kinds of situations are handled successfully on a case-by-case basis and don't require adding more "rules."

Ladder does, however, have several behaviors which cause immediate eviction: weapons in the home and physical confrontations with housemates. Other rules which, if unresolved, result in a 30-day eviction are: no smoking in the homes, non-payment of rent, and interrupting the safe and quiet enjoyment of others. While technically the use of alcohol and illegal drugs call for immediate eviction, the staff of Ladder attempts to work with residents to resolve these challenges and, if necessary, help the resident find a program that addresses these problems.

STATEMENT OF FAITH

"I was hungry and you gave me something to eat. I was thirsty and you gave me something to drink. I was a stranger and you invited me in. I needed clothes and you clothed me. I was sick and you looked after me. I was in prison and you came to visit me...I tell you the truth, whatever you did for one of the least of these brothers of mine, you did for me." Matthew 25:35-40

It is upon these words of Jesus that Ladder Homes was founded. We believe Ladder Homes are God's homes. God gave us the vision and operated in the hearts of God's people to provide the support necessary to build and operate our homes. Throughout the years it has been through God's guidance that we have grown and continue to be the hands and heart of God for our residents.

- Ladder does not screen potential residents in terms of their faith. Ladder does not force or mandate participation in any faith-based activities.
- Ladder does offer regular Bible studies for our residents led by staff.
- Ladder staff members encourage residents in their spiritual journeys, recognizing the importance of this aspect of their lives in managing their mental illness.
- Ladder staff and Board rely on their faith in God when making decisions regarding residents and the program as a whole.
- Ladder staff rely on their faith in interacting with residents, praying for the wisdom and compassion needed to empower these children of God to live in this world as productive citizens.

People with mental illness suffer not only from a devastating illness but from the stigma still prevalent in our society arising from ignorance and prejudice. These persons are, indeed, "strangers in our midst"—strangers that society is afraid of and, therefore, ignores. And that fear results in a prejudice which, like all prejudices, is unjustified and unacceptable in any of God's people. The result is that these special children of God are isolated and often not welcomed by the community of God's people. These modern day strangers are among those to whom God's people are called. Hebrew 13:2 states "Do not neglect to show hospitality to strangers, for by doing that some have entertained angels without knowing it." God also speaks about these strangers in Psalm 146:7-9, "The Lord sets the prisoners free; the Lord opens the eyes of the blind. The Lord lifts up those who are bowed down; the Lord loves the righteous. The Lord watches over the strangers; he upholds the orphan and the widow."

Ladder residents are among those whom God commands us to love: the oppressed, the hungry, the sick, the homeless, those in prison, the strangers among us. Ladder offers our residents affordable, appropriate housing and case management support which meets their needs. We give voice to their concerns and advocate for them when necessary. We empower them to become productive members of society. And we love them, recognize their worth as children of God, and, with God's help, walk with them on their journey to become all that God has created them to be.

A home—a haven where one can feel safe and accepted, where people can be encouraged and empowered to realize their full potential—this is the thesis of Ladder's story. Along with affordable, appropriate houses, support for the residents comes from the staff who serve as case managers and friends, helping in whatever way may be necessary and appropriate to empower each resident to be as independent as possible and to become a productive member of the community. Together the community volunteers, the residents themselves, the Ladder Homes Board of Directors and the support staff form the heart of Ladder. Out of this heart, houses have been transformed into homes and strangers into families. In such an environment those who too often have experienced rejection and pain, stigma and misunderstanding, can grow and blossom into the special, worthwhile people they are.

The residents of Ladder are intelligent, capable, creative people whose mental illness has robbed them of their dreams and the life they had planned to live. In the continuing chapter of Ladder's story, a tale is being told of an awakening hope for meaningful lives. One prolific artist has his work showcased in homes, churches, galleries and local businesses. Two residents have co-authored a book on their experience living with schizophrenia. Gardens at each location, planted and tended by residents, provide vegetables and flowers for their enjoyment and the enjoyment of others. One resident serves as the Ladder Maintenance Supervisor, working with volunteers and residents to maintain the houses and yards, while several others use their "jack of all trades" skills in several of the homes. Many of the residents hold down part-time jobs, work as volunteers in the community, or attend school. In all of this, their earlier dreams are gradually being replaced by new dreams, and lives without hope are finding new meaning, all of this made possible because of a home, a family, and support

Ladder is a great idea. As a resident I can honestly say that I really appreciate all that Ladder is doing for me.

When I was 15 years old, I was in the Kalamazoo Institution, and I told myself I was going to do something about this. It was my cry to God. I feel my prayers have been answered through Ladder. Ladder is committed to giving people outlets instead of being committed or put into foster care. Ladder is a God-send…it is much more humane…it takes everyone's individual needs into account instead of one role for everyone, which is the way it is in foster care or the hospital.

My favorite thing about Ladder is the visits from the Ladder case manager. Ladder is a step up to quality living. I feel that through Ladder God has helped me to accept my weaknesses and understand my strengths.

The folks I live with support me. I don't have to hide because of the stigma of mental illness. I am happy to be living with folks who understand me and who are able to put a different spin on things… give me a different perspective. I am glad to be living with people who know how it feels to live with mental illness.

Ladder has a homey feel to it. It gives each and every resident a chance to exercise who they are…to be everything they can be. It would be difficult for this to happen without the assistance of Ladder.

The support of other people is so very important for all of us. And that is why Ladder is so important for the folks who live here. Each one has a strong sense of support. Everybody cares for the other. It feels very comfortable and safe.

Before Ladder I was living on the streets and in shelters, totally unstable and without any home or family for support. Now I live at Ladder where I am free to be independent, yet know that I am safe because I have the support I need to be stable and as healthy as I can be.

My favorite thing about Ladder is to be able to sit in a cozy living room and hang out, watch TV, listen to music, and talk to different kinds of people.

Ladder's story is your story and my story—the story of a parent or a sibling, a friend or a colleague. We don't know how Ladder's story will end, but we know that it is a story worth telling—as worthwhile and special as the Ladder residents themselves.

There are times when I become frustrated, discouraged. In Ottawa County alone there are thousands of individuals who could benefit from our program. It works! Ladder provides the kind of housing and support that improves the quality of life for all of our residents. But for now we can only serve twenty-three individuals. Then I hear God's voice whisper to me, "Be faithful to what I have called you to do. You have been called to serve in your little corner of the world. Do it well with passion and love."

For me, Ladder is Jon David's legacy. Several years ago the first Ladder home was renamed the Jon David Miller Home in his memory. The pain of both his years of struggle and his death never completely go away. My comfort comes from knowing that out of my loss, out of his pain, others with mental illness have the opportunity to live a quality life and to dream new dreams. Voices of hope and advocacy still speak.

Part IV

Epilogue

THE VOICES STILL SPEAK

<u>VOICES OF LADDER STAFF</u>

My life changed the day I began working for Ladder, a non-profit organization that has its foundation built on friendship. It's a simple concept, but an amazingly profound difference maker for the case management of the individuals we have been blessed to serve. Ladder's mission is to provide affordable housing with supportive services – a successful combination for appropriate housing for adults with mental illness. However, the "secret ingredient" to our successful formula is friendship. Since 2005, I have witnessed this type of support transform life after life, including my own. As a case manager, you can put all the right supports in place for an individual, and then scratch your head and wonder why he or she is not moving forward. But when someone finds out that you truly care, a friendship is born – step one. Your extended hand is embraced and together you're walking forward – step two. The budding friendship grows stronger and you walk the journey together – step three and beyond!

Before coming to Ladder, I was an Associate Pastor of Youth Ministry for seven years. The most transformational part of youth ministry is the close friendships the youth pastor builds with the teens – hanging out together, going out to eat or a movie, spending time being available to the ones you have been called to serve. Bringing that availability to Ladder has led to bible studies, two trips to Chicago, two trips to Art Prize in Grand Rapids, Tulip Time in Holland, shopping, lots of coffee houses and restaurants (gaining weight), and tennis, racket ball, roller blading, and lots of walking (losing weight). Being present for someone today leads to a better tomorrow. The Ladder way includes taking the call, listening, caring and sharing, committing time, putting out the fire if necessary, and above all fulfilling God's commandment to love your neighbor as yourself.

The Ladder blessing is the generosity of our residents. A true friendship is a two way street – a give and take relationship. The residents have blessed and continue to bless my life and those around them daily. They have purchased meals and needed items for those who would have gone without, volunteered their time and skills in their own homes and within the community, and have made themselves available to those who needed them. They have taken control of their mental illness and have redefined what it means to live successfully. The residents have inspired me to redefine my life – to work even harder, to live my life fuller, and to recognize and appreciate God's daily blessings.

Jonathan Book

Ladder Executive Director/Case manager

2005-present

The name "Ladder" probably brings to mind vastly different feelings and memories for those of us that "did" Ladder, or still "do" Ladder, than for the average person. How does one "do" Ladder? In a phrase... 'with all your heart, soul, mind, and strength'. Is this wrongly using God's word? I don't believe so.

Ladder is a place brought about and blessed by God. It is a calling from God that requires full and complete commitment. Ladder is a reflection of a lifestyle of actively participating in the lives of others. The "others" God has called us at Ladder to happen to include the many individuals in the Ottawa County area that deal with the difficult symptoms of their mental illness every day, every week, for years upon years. God has called Ladder to walk with these individuals, to advocate for them and with them, to provide housing that is safe, secure, and actually affordable. Ladder encourages residents to see themselves as capable, and worthy of being respected. Ladder helps our residents to become involved in the community around them, to develop friendships, to participate in church, groups, and other activities that everyone else in the community participates in.

To choose to become part of Ladder is to involve everyone that you are connected with, whether that is your family members, your close friends, your community connections. You see, Ladder quickly becomes a passion, a God-given passion. Ladder staff are driven to do whatever it takes to help our residents remain stable and as symptom-free as possible, even if that means spending many hours waiting for the psychiatrist, or the crisis worker. Ladder residents are not put on the back burner, told to wait until tomorrow, next week, or their next scheduled appointment. They are valued, and are as family to us. Ladder regularly goes above and beyond when it comes to supporting our residents.

It does not matter that I have long moved away from West Michigan, and no longer actually work for Ladder. In fact, in whatever job I do, I still am "doing Ladder". The concept, and the commitment are ingrained in me no matter which mental health agency I find myself working for. Whether a person happens to have a mental illness, or has a chronic physical illness, or whether they are healthy, but deal with other difficulties in their lives, all are children of our Almighty God. All deserve to be loved, respected, encouraged, and highly valued. Nothing else is acceptable. In all that we do, we do as if we are doing it for the Father. Because we are.

Sue Van Peursem

Ladder Case Manager

7/1996-2005

VOICES OF PARENTS OF ADULT CHILDREN WITH MENTAL ILLNESS

Ladder helped to save my son's life and dignity. That is how I feel about Ladder. I owe the organization a huge dept. It also went far in saving his mom. When Scott began managing his illness, the biggest fear I dealt with was his having a safe place to live. I spent sleepless nights and many, many tears, desperate to help him find an alternative for when he would be released from care. My home was not an option at the time. When I heard about Ladder it was like someone opened a window to clear a smoke-filled room. I felt like

I could breathe again. I also joined NAMI and began the work of helping others like me, parents and family members dealing with the agony of coping with an adult child with mental illness. I treasure the friendships I have gained and hope that I can reconnect when I am able in years to come. I want to be a part of insuring the continuation of this housing alternative. It feels like more than housing. It feels like an extended family.

-Jill

At the age of 17 my son began to experience serious problems. It began with depression, then moved into mania, by which time his diagnosis became clear, namely bipolar illness (also referred to as manic depression).

Mental illness is always a huge shock in the life of the person and of his or her family. The terror, disorientation, desperation, sadness, near hopelessness, and chaos in our lives over the next 11 years are almost beyond description. During his worst years, my son was unable to do much that was "normal," including attending church. Having people come up to ask about how he was doing caused him to bolt to the closest exit. He stopped going to church

Thirty years later, and after more than a decade living with my son's mental illness, we became Catholics. We understand that those "dark" years are not lost to us. Instead, we believe that our suffering is taken up by Christ into his cross. We are now experiencing something like the resurrection, because God has honored our faith and hope with recovery and opportunities to share these blessings with others. My son is now able to encourage others—to comfort others with the comfort he has received from God, as St. Paul says.

I would never have asked God for the most difficult stretches of our journey. But the Lord knew that the good gifts he planned for us would become complete only in this way.

-Robin

My daughter was diagnosed with bipolar disorder at age 11. As a mom it was very difficult seeing my young child so ill. She tried to kill herself at this age. Then she was in and out of mental hospitals for the next few years.

I was dealing with my own guilt, blame, and anger. It was hard seeing other children out playing and mine in a mental hospital for three months. I also had two younger children. I felt like giving up, but I couldn't because of my other children.

Going through all this we need help and support because we're feeling all alone. We met other parents whose children were acting out with the same behaviors as our daughter. Hearing their stories helped us. At that point I realized it wasn't I, it was how ill our daughter was.

For the first year we had a wonderful counselor. At one hospital I was told my daughter's behavior was all my fault. After the first year we had to get a new counselor and that's when we started on a roller coaster with our lives. You are trying to trust the professionals, but they are blaming you. I was told to change myself overnight for my child. I wasn't to cry, react, just let her do what she wanted. I had just been told that she was the most ill of those in the mental ward. After she was home her acting out became worse. Her new couonselors and doctors continued to blame me. I was told by one doctor to hit my daughter in order to get her in foster care and that my other children wouldn't be taken away, only her. That was just devastating to me. Of course I didn't listen, but she was the professional. As time went on I continued to receive this kind of advice.

There is a stigma with mental illness. We actually lost friends because they didn't understand mental illness. I was told by friends and family that they could handle my daughter better than I couldl. These people hurt me so much and didn't realize how sick my daughter was or what she was capable of. Over the years of professionals and friends telling me that I was not doing things right, I felt all alone. Even with my husband helping me through all this I became very depressed. People can be so cruel and opinionated. My sister, however, was so positive and supportive through the years. She convinced me to geet help for my depression.

After fighting with the system about medication and treatment for my daughter for over ten years we found positive support. My daughter was around 26 years old when I first heard of Ladder Homes. My daughter was living with us and doing volunteer work. We knew she couldn't live on her own without a support system. She wasn't bad enough for an adult foster care home. She moved into an apartment with Ladder Homes. The first year she had a roommate. From then until now she lives in the apartment by herself. For the first time in years I could get off the roller coaster. The support from Ladder had made such a difference in our lives. I finally have positive help for my child. Also the "blame mom" is over. We finally have positive support for my family. If we need anything, Ladder Homes is right there to help. My daughter feels like Ladder is her second family. She is close to the people in her apartmenet complex. She wouldn't be where she is now without the help from Ladder. They are always there for the good and the bad times. Now I don't worry about my daughter and feel better about myself.

A few years ago my daughter had to get a new therapist. This woman is the opposite of the past therapists. She is so helpful and positive. I was scared to meet her because I didn't want to be blamed again. It was such a positive experience for me. She has really helped my daughter. At present I go in some of the sessions with my daughter. It is nice and different to be told you are a good mom. I still have a hard time believing her, but I am working on it.

At present my daughter is now 34 years old. She is still living at Ladder Homes. She is at a place in her life where she has never been. She still goes to therapy once a month. She has a steady boyfriend and hopes to be married in a few years. They would continue to live at Ladder Homes where she will continue to receive the support she gets now.

I haven't seen my daughter this happy and doing so well in so many years. I am so proud of her for all the hard work she has done to get where she is now. I feel scarred for life from the professionals and the system. At the same time I thank God every day for where we are now.

-Bev

VOICES OF PERSONS WITH MENTAL ILLNESS

It is not surprising that I suffer from a mental illness. My mother suffered from major depressive disorder. A cousin on the paternal side of my family has schizophrenia. My father has a mood or personality disorder. My paternal grandmother suffered from untreated depression for most of her life. Her father lived with a severe mental illness. My maternal great-great grandfather committed suicide. Obviously, l in my case, there is a genetic portion to my mental illness.

During my sophomore year in high school I experienced a profound depressive episode. In the fall of my senior year I had a manic episode and was hospitalized at a juvenile psychiatric facility. This marked the official end of my life as a "normal" person. Never again would my developmental experiences mirror my age cohorts; neither would my development have the same directionality. My skills at recruiting social resources for emotional needs were stunted. I couldn't function well cognitively for the last year of high school, partly because my medications had to be changed often in order to deal with my particular symptoms. Many caused me to gain weight. I don't remember the bulk of my senior year or the summer after. Add to this psychopathological cocktail a natural social awkwardness with my age peers and one gets the result: me at 18 starting college.

I began a freshman year at Hope College and was living in a dorm. It was winter, in the spring semester when I had had enough of medication-induced stupor I decided to discontinue my mood stabilizer and continue to take my antidepressant. This was the most foolish and destructive choice as a person with bipolar disorder.

The following are just a few of the behaviors I exhibited during this time.

- *I left the remains of my Taco Bell order at the doorstep of a student with whom I was irritated.*
- *During the first class of Behavior Disorders I announced that I had bipolar disorder. This was the last day I attended.*

- *I stayed up all night several or more nights in a row.*
- *On another winter night at 3:00 a.m. I walked home down the middle of the streets, got my Mom's car out of the garage, drove to Denny's, ate two full meals, drove to JP's to get coffee, sat to watch the sunrise in the parking lot, drove home, and dropped the car off before my mom awoke for work in the morning.*
- *I was mad one night and dropped a large stack of my CDs in the street while crossing. Several days later I saw an art student listening to one of them.*
- *During dinner at Phelps, I walked to a piano in the corner, and started "playing" chords and assorted notes until all students had left.*
- *Another night I got very mad, grabbed a long piece of wood and started to walk to my friend's house. When I reached the bronze girl on kitty-corner to Centennial Park I smashed the piece of wood on the face of the statue.*

When I was living at home, I would go to the basement and destroy my own paintings, easels, and shelves until I was exhausted. I broke windows and threw a banana against the living room wall. Often I walked the dunes with my dog Corey, found a suitable tree, a dozen or more fallen branches and cracked them against the trunk, one after another. This was the purpose of my visits. I remember Corey looking perplexed as he came back from exploring, found a place to sit, and watched.

The spring of 1999 was the last and only time I decided to stop taking my medication. In total, between the year of my diagnosis in

1997 and 2002 I was hospitalized about 7 times due to breakthrough and treatment-resistant symptoms. Each time in the hospital I felt a great empathy for my fellow patients, perhaps even more than any "self empathy."

Trying to remember the exact details of this time often feels like traveling to an alien land. Accessing certain negative memories, whether they be of academic failure or damaging relationships, can feel like this.

Despite never again wavering from my medication regiment, I was unable to successfully return to school in a sustained way until 2008. Between 2000 and 2006 I dabbled in taking one or two classes at a time, but it never worked. It wasn't until late in 2008 that I was able to begin thinking about re-enrolling in classes. By then functional stability had become well established (due to better treatment) and it allowed me to return to school and graduate this past December.

For the first time in my adult life, the future though unknown, tenuous, but also seems bright and promising. It has a variety of potential paths and filled with possibilities of various sorts of success and enterprise. This is both a matter of pride and a source of some anxiety. As I move forward, I travel slowly beyond college, the pace of life is undefined. Self-development and social orientation enter new stages. But I do not feel scared. With the help of God I move forward.

-Nathan

Beginning at age six I was abused by my father and my brother. I believe my childhood traumas resulted in my mental illness—depression, anxiety, sleep disorder, and panic attacks. I was all alone in my pain. When I had my first nervous breakdown, I had no one to support or help me. My doctor finally sent me to a psychiatrist and therapist who helped me understand what was going on. Without them I don't know what I would have done. In fact, it was only through therapy which finally convinced me that I would have to take medication for the rest of my life. During that time I cried for hours believing that I was indeed crazy like my family and friends told me. Several years later I had a second breakdown, worse than the first. But this time I knew what to do—get to my doctor and therapist. I didn't go into the hospital (still won't go) because I am claustrophobic and am afraid of getting locked up. I just basically lie in bed when things get too bad.

Today I have more support of friends, neighbors, and Ladder staff. I take my meds faithfully. I watch TV. I have people that I do things for. That's really important to me—helping people. But still, being mentally ill is tormentl. It makes me sad. I miss my mom. When my friends aren't around much, I miss them. When I get really sad I rock myself. Talking to people who understand me helps. I hate being alone. I wouldn't say I am content, but I have learned to live with my mental illness. My dreams are to have a husband, maybe a job, and financial security, but I don't expect those dreams to come true.

-Pam

A DISORIENTED JOURNEY
EXCERPT FOR A Friend

I sat Lotus just as my Tietan teacher did in her sleeping quarters. She posed the question "What would Enlightenment be for you?" I paused, and said "Like a rocket shooting straight up", she added "hmmmn". She went into a meditative silence as I sat quietly waiting. I felt in the ether through the walls surrounding the home come down the hallway a shadowy presence. She said "Did you fell that? That's the demon">

A year later far away, I was no stranger to the nuances of synthronicity and mental energies. I sat in my room alone when Spirit first spoke. Three guides then made their audible presence to me one male two female. This began a clairaudient communication that has always been with me since.

The energies of the presence were so profound. Time space warping and forming into a dream state that I was swept into within. Three weeks passed with such energies I found myself without food or sleep for two of those weeks. Such energies must have been learned from many past lives of practice.

If only my karma had been cleared before launching myself into space. I managed to sustain life in the altered state for more than a year. But trouble surfaced and whawt was a dream became the wake of a nightmare. A life time of recovery now lay before me.

But blessed are the ways of light, now nearing middle age putting behind me the distant past. Enlightenment has dawned and I have learned balance and the disciplining of my mind. I could be embarrassed that I was placed into the mental health system. But a humble laugh and smile within is plenty sufficient.

-Scott

Resources: Books and Websites

Books: Mental Illness

Bush, Max
Voices From the Shore
Dramatic Publishing
(A drama of a young person struggling to understand his mental illness)

Emmons, Stuart and Craig Geiser
Living With Schizophrenia
Court and Nelson

Fast, Julie A. and John D. Preston
Loving Someone With Bipolar Disorder
New Harbinger Publications

Helping Families Cope wiwth Mental Illness
(Edited by Harriet P. Lefley and Mona Wasow)
Harwood Academic Publishers

Jamison, Key Redfield
An Unquieet Mind
Vintage
(A memoir of moods and madness)

Johnson, Julie Tallard
Hidden Victims
Doubleday
(An eight-stage healing process for families and friends of the mentally ill)

McLean, Richard
Recovered, Not Cured
Allen and Unwin
(A journey through schizophrenia)

Miklowitz, David J.
The Bipolar Disorder Survival Guide
(What You and Your Family Need to Know)
TShe Guilford Press

O'Conner, Richard
Undoing Depression
Berkley Trade

Secunda, Victoria
When Madness Comes Home
Hyperion
(Help and hope for families of the mentally ill)

Shapiro, Joseph P.
No Pity
Random House
(People with disabilities forging a new civil rights movement)

Sheehan, Susan
Is There No Place On Earth For Me?
Vantage Books
(A true story of Sylvia Frumkin who suffers with schizophrenia)

Smith, Tom
A Balanced Life
(Strategies for coping with the mental health problems of a loved one)
Hazelden

Timmerman, John H.
A Season of Suffering
Multnomah Press
(One family's journey through depression)

Torrey, E. Fuller, M.D.
Nowhere To Go
Harper & Row
(The tragic odyssey of the homeless mentally ill)

Torrey, E. Fuller, M.D.
Surviving Schizophrenia
(A family manual)
Harper & Row

Vine, Phyllis
Families in Pain
Pantheon Books
(Children, siblings, spouses, and parents of the mentally ill speak out)

Voices of Bipolar Disorder
(The healing companion: stories for courage, comfort and strength)
(Edited by The Healing Project)
Lachance Publishing

Woolis, Rebecca
When Someone You Love Has a Mental Illness
Putnam Publishing Group
(A handbook for family, friends, and caregivers)

Books: Suicide, Death, Grief

Chance, Sue, M.D.
Stronger Than Death
(When suicide touches your life: a mother's story)
Avon Books

Fine, Carla
No Time to Say Goodbye
(Surviving the suicide of a loved one)

Grollman, Earl
Living When a Loved One Has Died
Beacon Press
(A unique journal providing a constructive approach to working through grief)

Larch, Cobain and Jean
Dying to Be Free
(A healing guide for families after suicide)

Lewis, C.S.
A Grief Observed
Bantam Books
(A book of rediscovered faith after the death of a loved one)

Wolterstorff, Nicholas
Llament For A Son
Wm. B. Eeerdman
(A simple, honest, expression of one man's grief following the death of his son)

Websites

www.nami.com
www.nimh.hib.gov
www.mentalhealth.com
www.schizophrenia.com
www.pslgroup.com
www.biplar.com
www.DBSAlliance.org
bipolar.about.com
www.ladderhomes.org